D. A. Martens

YALE LECTURES ON THE
RESPONSIBILITIES OF CITIZENSHIP

RESPONSIBILITY AND CULTURE

YALE LECTURES ON THE
RESPONSIBILITIES OF CITIZENSHIP

RESPONSIBILITY
AND CULTURE

BY

L. P. JACKS

PRINCIPAL OF MANCHESTER COLLEGE, OXFORD,
EDITOR OF "THE HIBBERT JOURNAL"

NEW HAVEN · YALE UNIVERSITY PRESS
LONDON · HUMPHREY MILFORD · OXFORD UNIVERSITY PRESS
MDCCCC XXIV

CONTENTS

RESPONSIBILITY AND CULTURE

THE ALLEGED SICKNESS OF CIVILIZATION

IN addressing you on "The Responsibilities of the Citizen," in accordance with the Dodge Foundation, I shall take it for granted that no question exists among us as to the reality of these responsibilities. The foundation of this Lectureship and the presence of so large an audience to hear the matter discussed prove, I think, that the responsibilities of the citizen are not only recognized but acutely felt.

The price we pay for gaining our *rights* as citizens is that we become aware, immediately, of our *responsibilities*. Our civilization has reached that stage. The process of winning our rights, though not complete, has advanced sufficiently far to give us at least a dawning sense of our duties—a phenomenon full of promise for the future of mankind. This dawning sense of duty must be given a closer definition, expanded into a fuller knowledge, and into a more faithful practice.

It is through their subsequent transformation into duties that our rights become significant. Rights which remain arrested at that stage are like fruit that has never ripened—"green plums from the garden of Beelzebub," to borrow a phrase of John Bunyan's. They have evil effects. Or we may compare them to the brains of cretins which cease to grow at the stage of infancy. A community possessed of rights which had failed to grow into duties would be socially imbecile. The rights of the members would be worthless; their liberty, a sham; their government, if they had one, the laughing-stock of the world.

Autocracy makes the mistake of imposing duties on the citizen without giving him the corresponding rights. Democracy gives him his rights to begin with; but always in the expectation that he will develop them into duties. When this development fails, as it easily may and sometimes does, the end of democracy is disaster. In certain countries of Europe, for example, notably in Italy and Spain, there has been of late a serious setback to the democratic principle, the cause of which, if closely examined, lies in the failure of the citizens of those countries to translate their rights into duties. Freedom means just that, as Mazzini taught. The only real freedom is that which uses the possession of rights as an opportunity for the performance of duty. If the Statue of Liberty in New York Harbour means anything less than this, it ought to be removed.

To the task of defining our duties I now address myself, not without a due appreciation of its difficulties. It is easy to discuss these things at great length—many people are now doing so—but difficult to discuss them in a manner that makes any real difference to the lives of those who take part in the discussion. One of the most disconcerting facts, in these times, is the flagrant disproportion that exists between the enormous amount of propaganda, on more or less idealistic lines, concerning our duties and their bearing on the fortunes of civilization, and the almost imperceptible difference that it makes to the actual conduct of governments and of individual citizens. We exert ourselves greatly in the discussion of these things, in talk about them, but the change of heart and of conduct which ought to follow from these exercises is not easy to detect. They leave the governments standing pretty much where they were, and the individual as much inclined as ever to indulge his anti-social habits. Much of this propaganda is what Carlyle called "cant."

We are to think, then, not of what the citizen may get out of society in the way of benefit, but of what his duty requires him to give in the way of service. And our thinking, if it is to be of any value, must take a line which leads into corresponding action. A discussion which merely leads on to a further discussion,—which is what "free" discussion generally amounts to in these days,—a book which merely provokes the writing of another book, either by the same author or by one of his critics, will not meet the wants of any of us who may happen to be in earnest about our responsibilities, but will merely swell the torrent of unprofitable talk, which, as I have said, is already swollen out of all proportion to the actual result in human conduct—in the policy of governments and in the daily habits of the citizen.

To whom, or to what, are we responsible? What is the 'society' to which our duties are owed? The answer is, obviously, we owe them in the first instance to the nation under whose government we live and of which we are members.

"My country first" is a perfectly sound motto, so far as it goes. It becomes vicious only when the "first" is also taken as the "last." Though the responsibilities of the citizen *begin* with his own country, they do not *end* there; and if we treat them as ending there, we have a very imperfect conception of what they are, and the services we render to our own fellow citizens will be impaired accordingly. The duty we owe to our own country must be viewed in relation to the similar duties which the citizens of other countries owe to theirs; otherwise we shall not render to our own country the service it claims from us. Nationalism and internationalism are not antithetic terms. They mutually support one another. The best nationalists I have known were also the best internationalists. It is only in their lower forms that the two things stand opposed; when, for example, nationalism takes the form of collective selfishness, and when internationalism is a mere passion for world uniformity, for standardization in the lives of all nations. The higher internationalism values the diversity of gifts among the nations; and encourages each to stand firm on the distinctiveness of its own particular contribution to the common service of civilization. "My country first," then; but first only in the sense that it is here, in the country to which I belong, that the service must *begin* which I owe to mankind at large. By viewing my national duties in this light, they will indeed take a wider range, and acquire a deeper stringency, but that will only raise the value of the distinctive service which my own country renders to the world, without in the least impairing its distinctiveness, or weakening my effectiveness as a patriot.

Nay, more. Any conception of social duty which stands arrested at the national boundary, and owns no responsibilities beyond that, is bound to end in the *disservice* of the country in whose in-

terest it stands so arrested. Of late, indeed, there
has grown up a notion, not confined to one side
of the Atlantic, that great empires, if sufficiently
organized for the purpose, can play their parts as
self-contained units, independent of the foreigner,
who may be allowed to go to the devil, or otherwise, at his pleasure. It is a tempting theory,
which many hollow plausibilities combine to support. But in truth it is no more practicable now
than would be a return to the walled cities of the
Middle Ages. The individualities of nations need,
indeed, to be preserved, but the only way to pre-
serve them, under existing conditions, is to unite
them in reciprocal service. The attempt to keep
them self-contained will lead to war, either actual
or suppressed, and so to the destruction of the
distinctive national values which we ought to aim
at preserving. We are preparing disaster for our
country just in so far as we seek to withdraw her
from the path of reciprocal service. Under modern
conditions there is no other way by which the
distinctiveness of any nation can be preserved.

Our responsibilities, then, are to civilization at
large, and to our own country so far as we believe,
as all of us do believe, that it has a distinct contribution of its own to make to the cause of human
progress in general.

But our responsibilities to civilization at large

cannot be determined until our minds are made up as to the general value of the civilization in which we find ourselves living. It is *industrial* civilization that now confronts us. Is it worth preserving? Does our duty require us to join in efforts for its preservation? Shall we treat it as a station on the road to something better? Or is it moving on the wrong road altogether, and shall we find our duty, not in efforts for its preservation, but in efforts for its destruction, for clearing it out of the way and replacing it with another type of civilization, more after the heart's desire?

Both opinions are widely held at the present day. They are sometimes held by the same thinker according as he is in one mood or another. Mr. Bertrand Russell, for example, in his recent book, *The Prospects of Industrial Civilization,* after describing a very comprehensive scheme for the development of industrial civilization on its present lines, as a thing worth preserving, confesses to moments when he would welcome the advent of a comet to end the whole performance for good and all. Obviously we cannot determine the value of our responsibilities as citizens so long as it is an open question with us whether or no industrial civilization is worth while.

I propose to narrow the scope of the inquiry, since the general form of it is far too comprehensive to be dealt with in the time at my disposal. I would bring it to a point in this question: Our western civilization—is it sick or is it healthy?

If sick, our responsibilities to it will take the form of finding the appropriate medical remedies, of performing the appropriate surgical operations, or possibly of ending it altogether as a thing incurably diseased. All these operations are in fact being advocated by persons who have started from the assumption that civilization is sick, perhaps without criticizing what they have assumed.

If healthy, then our reforming activities will take another line and display a very different temper; and our whole conception of social responsibility will be profoundly affected.

I propose to take the question in this narrow form, and I venture to think that the answers we get will be found applicable to any wider form of the question in which we may be interested.

In the manifold types of social propaganda now active two main streams of tendency may be clearly distinguished.

One is dominated by the idea that our civilization is a sick patient, afflicted with many maladies, which are mostly those of old age, and which can only be dealt with by curative or remedial measures. Wherever this tendency is dominant, the demand arises for great public operations, sometimes of a summary character, to be carried out by legislative enactment.

The other tendency treats society as though it were a growing and healthy organism whose interests are best served by educational activities. The two tendencies are frequently intermingled in a very confusing way. The revolutionist and the educationalist are at odds with one another; and often the two tendencies may be found in the same individual.

As things now are, it seems to me that the analogy of the sick patient has the firmer hold on our minds. I do not mean that the image of the growing organism has been definitely dismissed from the field of social reform. In all countries there is a great and increasing interest in education—a sure sign that the conception of civilization as still young and healthy is asserting itself. But though the interest in education is great, the interest in *remedies* seems to be far greater. Throughout the whole of the western world, not more, I think, in the old part of it than in the new, there is a deeply rooted belief that the ills from which civilization is suffering can be cured by appropriate legislative enactment—which faith bears a very close psychological resemblance to the notion many people have that all diseases can be cured by appropriate physic. There are various words ending in 'ism' which are being extensively advocated as the cure-alls of civilization, and which I can never hear without finding myself in the atmosphere of a doctors' clinic, or of a drug store. In some of these 'isms' one can detect a distinct smell of chloroform; but others are more innocent. And besides this general faith in the efficacy of legislative physic, to be selected and administered by majority voting, there crops up from time to time a very curious and interesting phenomenon—the belief, namely, in the advent of a social messiah, whose office it will be to compose the master prescription, the all-conquering 'ism,' the mere repetition of which will restore civilization to health. At the present moment, indeed, many persons are going about who claim to have discovered the panacea in question. Their place is among the vendors of patent medicines, whose methods of advertisement they copy.

As to the causes which have led to the conception of society as a sick patient in need of "remedies," I shall have something more to say later on. For the present, we may regard it as a by-product of the habit of self-scrutiny, which Carlyle set down among the chief "characteristics" of the modern age, and which, since his time, has greatly strengthened its hold, not on individuals alone, but on nations, and on civilization as a whole.

Up to a certain point self-scrutiny, no doubt, is a wholesome exercise. But the point is soon reached; beyond it our conclusions are almost inevitably false and the results morbid. The wisdom of self-scrutiny is to be content with the minimum. But psychology, both social and individual, asks for the maximum and in these days we are all psychologists or ambitious to become so. Whence the conclusion that something deadly is the matter with us, with its inevitable sequel in the vogue of the soul-doctor and of the social quack. These people flourish; but it is greatly to be doubted whether anybody else is deriving much benefit from the habit to which men and nations have now become addicted, and no nation more so than the American, of staring at themselves in the moral looking glass. For the saying holds true, both of individuals and of whole societies that 'the healthy know not of their health, but only the sick.'

Social literature, on both sides of the Atlantic, not excluding that part which is contributed by novelists and playwrights, bears witness to what I am saying. Taken as a whole, this literature, which has now grown to vast proportions, is not cheerful reading. The prevalent note is one of alarm, verging toward despair. We have a class of writers in England, and I think the same class is not unknown in America, who seem to glory in exhibiting the appalling mess we have made of things. "The total depravity of modern society" would be a fair description of their doctrine—the Gospel of Jonathan Edwards translated into its social equivalents.

Since the war this kind of thing has of course been greatly on the increase. As one who felt the war pretty close to him, I have sometimes thought that not the least of its horrors is the use that has been made of it as an argument for lowering the self-respect of civilization. The war has been exploited by professional pessimists and by social quacks. The vices of an age, like the vices of an individual, are apt to get written on brass, its virtues in water. In the one case, as in the other, the voice of calumny can always find a theme. Of course, the semblance of the thing was all against a high estimate of human nature, and still remains so. In the war, and in what has followed since, there was much to make our civilization greatly ashamed of itself.

But the supreme test of human qualities lies in a region which is apt to be overlooked by superficial observers. It is the capacity that men have and that nations have for the endurance of suffering, the silent heroism that shuns publicity and seldom lifts up its voice in the streets. By that test let us judge before we declare, as some have been declaring of late, that the moral forces have failed. The war was a time of suffering—not of physical pain alone but of moral agony—such as civilization had never faced before—a veritable Golgotha for many nations. When we ask ourselves how it was faced—how it was endured—how it is being endured at this moment, for the suffering still goes on—the answer comes out in a form that ought to fill us not only with admiration for our human kindred, but with a boundless confidence in its future. There have been many sinister phenomena; there are many at this moment; but I doubt if civilized society has ever shown a sublimer courage under the stroke of calamity, a more inflexible patience in carrying its burdens, than we have witnessed during the last ten years. The ruin that has fallen upon Europe is frightful: but nowhere does the disposition exist to accept ruin as final, not even in those countries that have suffered most. Everywhere the spirit of the nations is facing their reverses with heroic valour, summoning the resources of intellect and will to retrieve the situation, sorely perplexed, indeed, but not unto despair. A civilization which shows that quality will not easily suffer itself to relapse into the Dark Ages, as some of our professional pessimists are now beginning to prophesy. It is this more than anything else—this fortitude of the nations under the test of suffering, this power of standing up to a great reverse, which convinces me that society is sound at heart. The time has not yet come to order a coffin for modern civilization.

This view, as I have said, receives little encouragement from the great host of social critics, doctors and pathologists, who are now busy in "diagnosing" our condition. The prevailing diagnosis leans toward deep-seated disease. Or rather, the disease is assumed before diagnosis begins and the only question is as to the name that is to be given it.

But we need to be doubly on our guard at that point; first against the tendency to indulge in sick fancies, for which our dabblings in psychology are largely responsible, and then against the various denominations of social practitioners, mostly quacks, who exploit our sick fancies in the literary interest. What these people have to say, most of us, by this time, know by heart, and some of us are growing a little tired of it. Their conception of society is that of a sick thing, stricken by one 'ism' and curable by another. The favoured terms of their pathology are materialism, scepticism, mechanism, industrialism, commercialism, capitalism, nationalism, while the "remedies" range through a long list from communism at the one end to fundamentalism at the other. Now and then the social pathologist gets a chance to practise what he preaches, a turn of events places him in power, and a whole community, as in Russia, falls under the frightful tyranny of his 'treatment'—with what results we may now contemplate at our leisure.

Of all the dangers threatening civilization, the supremacy of the social quack doctor, masquerading as an "expert," is perhaps the greatest. The valetudinarian temper is widespread; recourse to legislative drugs, as the prime means to social health, is well established, and the constant failure of this "medicine" to yield the desired result is stimulating demand for stronger doses, instead of teaching us, as it should do, to abjure, once for all, the bad habit of interpreting our social fortunes in terms of "diseases" and "remedies." Thus, though we of the West have not fallen a prey to the social quack, as Russia has, we have at least fallen into a condition which is highly favourable to his operations. We need to remind ourselves that sociology is, as yet, an infant science; that social pathology is a non-existent science, and perhaps an unnecessary one; that all professions of exact knowledge in that department are fraudulent, that the "remedies" offered are guesswork, more likely than not to undermine the very fabric of our civilization, which is founded, not on "remedies," but on common sense, kind feeling, and honest work.

We have now taken what seems to me the necessary first step in the attempt to define our responsibilities as citizens. The first step is to dismiss from our minds the conception of civilization as a sick thing in need of remedies, and to substitute for that the conception of a half-grown thing in need of education. It would be a momentous change, affecting the whole character of the process which now goes under the name "reconstruction"—not a very happy name, since most of the things it is proposed to reconstruct are *growths,* which were not constructed in the first instance and cannot be reconstructed now. By making education the keynote of our efforts to improve the world, we should get rid at a stroke of those mechanical methods of thought which now impede us, at every turn, in the right handling of human affairs, and which are most insistent wherever the fortunes of civilization are interpreted in terms of disease and remedies.

Into the profounder implications of the change there is now no time for me to enter. I must content myself with suggesting a form of social service which those who agree with what I have said may embark upon at once—that of helping to disperse the sick fancies, the bad dreams, the nightmare pessimisms which are haunting the minds of men in these days, and providing so favourable an atmosphere for the operations of the social quack. These dreams and fancies are perilous stuff. They are lowering the social vitality and inducing diseases where, but for them, none would exist. To help society in clearing that stuff from its bosom is to play the part of a real benefactor. That civilization is worth while, that it is worth our while to make the best of it, that the best attainable is worth all the effort we can contribute to its attainment, these are the essential beliefs of the social worker, but impossible so long as our minds are dominated by the conception of the sick patient. Among the responsibilities of citizenship, none ranks higher than this—that we attack the sick fancies of our time and make it our business to put courage and confidence into the hearts of our fellow citizens.

But this we shall not be able to do till we have seen more deeply into the root and origin of what we are attacking. This we shall find where Carlyle, long ago, taught us to look for it—in the notion, which all men hold in these days, and encourage one another in holding, *that everybody has the right to be happy.* "Does not the whole wretched-ness," writes Carlyle, "the whole *Atheism,* as I call it, of man's ways, in these generations, shadow itself for us in that unspeakable Life-philosophy of his: The pretension to be what he calls 'happy'? Every pitifulest whipster that walks within a skin has his head filled with the notion that he is, shall be, or by all human and divine laws ought to be 'happy.' . . . The only happiness a brave man ever troubled himself with asking much about was, happiness enough to get his work done."

Now it is as certain as anything can be in this world that if we base our expectations on the no-tion that we have the right to be happy, we shall come to grief; we shall never get our 'right' ac-knowledged, neither by our fellow men nor by the laws and realities of the universe. This oft-told tale I do not here propose to enlarge upon. It is another aspect of the matter that now concerns us—that if we base our social criticism, our 'diag-nosis,' of civilization on that notion, judging the success and failure of man's adventure on this planet by the amount of "happiness" it has yielded him up to date, or is yielding him now, we in-evitably come to the conclusion that his adventure has miscarried, and we fall into line with the prophets of a sick civilization. Judged by the standard of "happiness" civilization never has been, is not, and never will be a success, and—I will venture to add—was never intended to be, by the wise powers which order its destinies. Yet there are few social writers of our time who have any other standard to apply to the matter in hand.

The doctrine of the 'Greatest Happiness' propounded by Bentham as a principle of legislation, transformed by the Mills into a principle of ethics, and subsequently denounced by Carlyle as "a very paltry speculation," has now virtually vanished from the high places of philosophy. But though officially discredited it has left a considerable deposit in the general mind.

First you have the assumption, to which I have just referred, that man has a right to be happy, so that, if he should chance to be unhappy, he has some kind of grievance to complain of against the universe or against his fellow men.

Behind this there is another notion, seldom expressed in so many words, but implicit in the morbid literature of our time, and intensely active in social speculation generally. It refers to the nature of the human individual. The idea seems to be that a human being, a living man or woman, is a cunningly devised contrivance for the production of happiness, so that man not only has the right to be happy, but has been designed by his Creator for that very purpose; his body with its

various organs, and his mind with its senses, instincts, desires, and passions being constructed
for the production in sufficient quantity of that
particular commodity we call 'happiness.'

Such is the conception of the individual human
being. Out of it there arises a parallel conception
of society, of the social system, which philosophers
tell us is the human individual writ large. The social system is regarded as a more extensive and
complicated contrivance for producing the same
article on a larger scale, or, as one might say, for
the mass production of happiness. Whence it follows, of course, that any social system which fails
to turn out happiness on the scale desired has
failed in the purpose for which it exists, and must
accordingly be condemned to the scrap heap or
at least "reconstructed." If we turn to that class
of writers who emphasize the diseased condition
of civilization, and ask for the facts on which
they base their alarming diagnosis, we find, in nine
cases out of ten, that the fact to which they point
is the deficient output in the matter of 'happiness.'
Thus Mr. Bertrand Russell, when he comes to the
question 'what makes a social system good or
bad?' at once pitches on the happiness produced
as the most important test. The social system is
to be judged good or bad, healthy or diseased, according to its record as a happiness factory, just

as the individual life, yours or mine, is a success or a failure according to the amount of happiness it yields to its possessor.

Now in considering these notions, which are widely prevalent, it will be enough if we confine attention to that part of the human individual which consists of his living body. I am not a physiologist, but I have a certain acquaintance with the human body derived from the fact that I possess one myself; and I have to confess that at no point of my bodily structure can I detect the slightest evidence that it has been constructed for the production of happiness—of happiness, I mean, in the sense of smooth-flowing enjoyment. I find a good deal in my body that seems to have been designed for the endurance of suffering, for bearing heavy burdens, for doing irksome and difficult operations, and for carrying me through dangerous places. The eye, for example, was clearly not planned for seeing only pleasant things, but for seeing anything that turns up; and so with all the other senses.

My doubts about happiness increase when I turn to the nervous system. If God intended that for pleasure I wish He had made it a little less sensitive. Every fiber in it is a permanent possibility of pain. As an instrument for the avoidance of pain I cannot conceive of anything less suited to the purpose than my nervous system.

But the greatest doubt of all comes from another fact which youth may disguise from itself, but which older men have to look in the face. These bodies of ours are constructed for dying as well as for living. They have the sentence of death written over every part of them. The death of the body is prefigured in every one of its living functions. A queer arrangement, that, to set up in a happiness factory. No, I cannot persuade myself that this body has been created or evolved with a view to affording its owner the maximum of smooth-flowing enjoyment. Nor can I persuade myself that the social system, which is only the individual writ large, has come into being for any such purpose. And I am glad it is so. For, after all, this happiness-hunting is a paltry business, unworthy of man, unworthy of civilization.

And if this is true of man's body, what shall we say of his mind? Can anyone who has considered the meaning of the terms he uses, seriously maintain that the mind of man, the soul of man, has its proper function in promoting enjoyment and in producing it? Surely the cynic is right when he advises us to stop *thinking* as the first and indispensable condition of a 'happy' life. It would be wise to stop *loving* also; for on that road there are tragic interruptions in store for all of us, which we can only avoid by keeping clear of "entangling alliances" in the love department. They will be sundered by an ineluctable stroke, and the cry will rise *de profundis,*

> "Oh for the touch of a vanished hand
> And the sound of a voice that is still."

Let none of us imagine that the reign of universal love, if ever it arrives on this planet, will find all men smiling. Their smiles, no doubt, will be more radiant; but their tears also will be hotter. It may well be questioned whether 'happiness' will be more abundant then than now.

I have dwelt on this matter because it seems to me the chief obstacle blocking the line of thought for which I am anxious to enlist your interest. We are in no condition for facing our responsibilities as citizens until our minds are swept clean of this wretched happiness-philosophy and of its morbific deposits. So long as we suffer it to dominate our thinking, which we still do in spite of professorial disclaimers, our doctrines of education, of labour, of social reform, of religion, are vitiated at the source. Above all, we shall misconstrue the meaning of liberty, taking it in the negative sense of mere freedom from restraint, in order that we may enjoy ourselves after our own folly, instead of in the positive sense—of willing subjection to an end that is worth while. For liberty also is a great responsibility, a responsibility to use our freedom from restraint as an opportunity for self-mastery, so that a man may say, 'Now that I have no master the time has come when I must be master of myself'—the process of binding the lower self in the interests of the higher, and the higher in the interests of the highest.

But now you will be asking 'If man was not made for happiness, for what was he made?' I will try to answer that in my next lecture.

IN the last lecture, I suggested that the idea of civilization as diseased is getting a dangerous hold. The dangers are (1) that the mind of society becomes unwholesomely inverted upon itself, like that of a valetudinarian who is constantly feeling his pulse and taking his temperature with a clinical thermometer; (2) that we come to rely upon remedies, upon legislative drugs, and so contract the social drug-habit; (3) that we suffer ourselves to be exploited by quacks, who make a living out of our fears.

While admitting that functional disorders of a grave kind exist, I cannot accept the theory of organic disease. In evidence that this theory is not sound I cited the extraordinary powers of endurance which the nations of the world displayed in the late disastrous war, and are still displaying in the disastrous peace which followed it. Believing that man is made as much for the endurance of pain as for the avoidance of it, I submitted that our civilization, under a test of pain as severe as any we can conceive, has come bravely off and proved its mettle, which a diseased civilization could hardly have done. I then went on to argue that the theory of a diseased civilization has its origin in certain paltry notions about happiness, and about man's right to be happy, which have held their ground in popular thought in spite of discredit in the high places of philosophy. A human being, I said, is not to be thought of as created for the small-scale manufacture of happiness, nor society as created for mass production of that ambiguous article.

At the end of all this, I was left with a formidable question. If man is not created for the production of happiness what, in heaven's name, is he created for? To this question I now address myself.

No originality in this matter is now possible. The question before us was answered some twenty-three centuries ago, in a perfectly intelligible and profoundly significant manner, by Aristotle.

The business of philosophy is not so much to explain things, as to find the things that explain themselves. This last is by far the more difficult operation of the two—at least it demands a higher order of genius. In our time we have grown so accustomed to approaching our problems through a fog of abstractions—such as 'mind' and 'matter,' for example—that the thing which explains itself has become impossible to find. In many cases, indeed, the fog has reached such a point of

there, standing erect, alert and ready, with the fire of life radiating from his person, with all his powers, aptitudes, capacities, and versatilities imprinted on his body and expressed on his countenance. Aristotle looked him up and down; examined the attitudes and parts of him one by one; his upright carriage, his eye gazing into the distance, his lips breaking out into speech, and above all his hands, his wonderful hands with their five mysterious fingers. Then, putting the parts together, he took in the vision as a whole, deeply meditating on the object before him; and finally, with a directness rare in philosophy, he asked himself this question,—What is that fine creature *for?* What does the cut of him betoken? What does the make-up of him suggest? Happiness? Smooth-flowing enjoyment? Not at all! That fine creature is for *action*. With that keen eye of his, looking out into the distance for opportunities, with that alert figure ready to start forward, with those five mysterious fingers eager for occupation, and with all the rest of him, who can doubt for a moment that this creature was meant for *action* —for undertaking difficult enterprises, for embarking on long expeditions by sea and by land, for achieving the highest excellence on a thousand roads, for enduring tremendous strains and protracted vigils, for sweeping and majestic operations, for standing hard knocks from fate and from circumstance—aye, and for giving hard knocks in return? Action the end of him! Action the meaning of him! Action is what the fine creature is *for!* It came in a flash, and down went the first principle of Aristotle's anthropology—*the end of man is an action.*

Compare that with the "paltry speculation" about happiness which arose in England about the time of that disreputable monarch Charles II, and afterward spread like a poisonous miasma over both sides of the Atlantic,—"happiness our beings' end and aim." Compare it, you young men, and make your choice. Take it with you into the abodes of luxury and idleness and tell it out to the people there who are bored to death. Arm yourselves with it when the quack doctors come along with their remedies for "unhappiness." Remember it when you are unhappy yourselves, as no power on earth can prevent you from being sometimes, and let it silence your complaints, whether they be against the universe or against your fellow men. The end of man is an action!

When Aristotle had finished with the individual he turned to the state. Or rather, he began discoursing about the state, for he had been thinking about it all the time he had been looking on the individual and asking himself what the fine creature was for. He had seen the state prefigured in that individual—another fine creature, growing out of the first and again entering into him as the principle of his action, and helping his action to keep true to its appointed path—which is the pursuit of excellence in everything that his hand or his brain finds to do. The state, for Aristotle, is, in essence, an educational enterprise, just as it was for Plato. What else can it be when he defines it as "a means to good life," as a principle entering into the life blood of the citizen and helping him not to live only, but to live *well*—a different thing from the happiness factory which the social doctors of today expect the state to be, and condemn it as diseased for not being?

I have sometimes wondered what Aristotle would say if he were to come to life again and inspect the modern state as we are trying to run it in these days. What form would *his* "diagnosis" take? "The trouble of your state, of your social system," he would say, "comes from the fact that for a long time past you have been trying to run it as a happiness factory, which it can never be and was never meant to be. But there is nothing fundamentally wrong with it—no fatal disease. The part which helps you to live the good life is still there, the principle is still at work. Develop that part of it, the educational part, the human-

istic part, cease thinking of the state as a physic
shop for providing you with remedies for your unhappiness, and you will find in a generation or two
that you have better states and better relations
between states than have ever existed before."

There is only one thing more I have to say about
Aristotle, and it is by way of answering a possible
criticism. "Aristotle," the critic will say, " is not
so indifferent to happiness as you make out. Is
there not a thing called εὐδαιμονία which he
promises to those who live the good life? And
what, pray, is εὐδαιμονία but happiness—smooth-
flowing enjoyment?"

I answer, it is nothing of the kind. Ἐνδαιμονια
means "good demonship." And the matter is just
this: that if you live a good life you will have
a good demon; you will be a well-demoned or
εὐδαίμων man. And what will your good demon
do for you? Well, he will open your eyes. He will
teach you to look into the heart of the fact. He
will give you those flashes of intuition which re-
veal the reality of things. He will guide you in
hitting the mark. Your good demon will correct
you; he will correct the distortions of your vision,
and you will be 'happy' in the sense that the man
is 'happy' whom the Lord correcteth. You will
find reality. You will hit the mark. Live the good
life, then, and this εὐδαιμονία, this good demon-

ship, this constant correction by the Lord, shall most assuredly be yours. The man blessed with a good demon, said the pagan; the man blessed with the fellowship of the Holy Spirit, said the Christian.

With this doctrine before us, this ancient doctrine of man as a being made for activity, and of society as a means to improving the quality of his actions, let us now translate it into terms appropriate to the industrial civilization of our time. That can be done in a sentence. The activity through which men and nations are now to realize themselves, is the thing we call *labour,* the actual contribution which each of them is making, by the work of the body or the work of the mind, to the value of the common life. Man, a creator of values; labour as the activity through which those values are to be created; the state as a means of educating and organizing his labours so that real values may come out at the end of them; this is the conception of man, and of the state, that I now commend to you in place of that other and debased conception—of man as made for happiness, and of the state as a contrivance for the mass production of that article.

If you accept the substitution, what follows? It follows that your responsibilities as a citizen will focus on the duty of making your life, through

your labour, productive of real value, and of helping your fellow citizens to use their lives in the
same manner. How that may be done best I shall
explain more fully in my lecture on Education—
for it is obviously an educational enterprise that
is here involved. Enough for the moment if we are
clear on the general principle, and see the immense expansion of social duty, and feel the
deeper sense of responsibility that follows from it.
Social duty is no longer a mere question of making the right use of your vote for the promotion
of happiness. It becomes the question of making
the right use of your whole personality, of your
whole life, and of helping others to do the same,
for the creation of real value. Your vocation,
whatever it may be, is now the great field of social
service, in which, through the labour that has
fallen to you, you make your contribution of ex-
cellent performance. The well doing of everything
that needs to be done is now your motto, and the
motto of the entire community of which you are
a member.

I offer you that as the translation into terms
appropriate to our highly complex industrial civilization of Aristotle's doctrine that the end of man
is activity—the well doing of everything that
needs to be done, on the great field of human
labour. I offer it as indicating the only possible

line on which industrial civilization can advance
to better things. When its significance has been
fully grasped, and when all that botheration about
"happiness" has been finally got rid of, we shall
be in the way to a renaissance, to a great revival
—a revival of the arts, to begin with—for art is
nothing else than the well doing of what needs to
be done; then a revival of morality—for there
can be no sound morality while men are scamping
their jobs; and, lastly, a revival of religion,—because there can be no religion which is not in its
essence a religion of work,—a dedication of one's
life to the pursuit of excellence in all the labours
belonging to our place in the social complex.

It is not the labour of any particular class, such
as the manual workers, that we are here concerned
with, but the labour of the whole community in
the endless variety of occupations, from the
simplest to the most highly specialized, from dig-
ging in the ground to governing the state, from
the bench of the carpenter to the operating table
of the surgeon, from the stokehold of the ship,
where men are shovelling coals into a furnace, to
the studio of the artist, where things of beauty are
being created. We need to think of all that as
though it were a single whole, but a whole made
up of an immense number of functions, which are
not really separate, but all connected and mutu-

ally dependent, all united and woven together with the general task of carrying on the life of society from year to year and from century to century. The whole community may be considered as though it were a single labouring unit, with ten thousand different tasks distributed among its members, all linked together into the one common task which we call civilization. Looking at labour in that synoptic manner, one may say, in homely language, that society has only one job to offer to its members. The name of it is civilization, or, if you prefer, progress. We may be farmers or statesmen, carpenters or surgeons, stokers or artists, teachers, lawyers, shopkeepers, clergymen— what you will; but these vocations are only the different names we have for our different contributions to the one task we all share in common, that of carrying forward the work of civilization, which is the work of the ages, and which some call the Kingdom of God.

It is a fruitful way of looking at the matter. For certain purposes, of course, we have to look at labour piecemeal, to consider its different varieties one by one. But when we have done that, when we have analyzed labour into the various trades and callings, and considered what is due to each, then we need to bring them all together again, and see them combining with one another into the unitary task which society as a whole has to accomplish, the vision of the world's labour as a unitary operation. In that way we shall see what a tremendous task we are confronted with in these days—that, namely, of keeping the good which civilization has won already and then carrying it on to something better; we shall see this task demanding from each of us the uttermost of his strength and his courage; each separate function will be ennobled by this vision of the great whole to which it contributes; we shall be more anxious to make our own work a real contribution to it, and not a sham one; and above all we shall be more ready to value the contributions which other men and other nations are making, and without which our own would not be possible. The more that view of the matter sinks into our minds the more unwilling we shall be to waste our energies in mutual quarrels and in wars, and the more eager we shall become to devise means of co-operation, of pulling together.

Conceiving labour, then, as the "action" through which industrial civilization is to realize whatever higher possibilities are hidden within it, let us now ask what leisure is, and how it stands related to the general responsibilities of the citizen.

Leisure is commonly thought of in terms which represent it as the opposite of labour, as a state when responsibility approaches the vanishing point, when exertion ceases and the worker gives himself up to rest and enjoyment. In the hours of labour we do our duty; in the hours of leisure we have no duty but abandon ourselves to impulse and inclination.

There is an element of truth in this conception, especially in the emphasis it lays on the necessity of rest. But if taken as the whole truth about leisure it leads to conclusions which are absurd and disastrous.

So far as leisure means the state of having nothing to do, of having no duties to perform but only inclinations to follow, there is no prospect that leisure will ever become the general lot of mankind. The indications point in the opposite direction. If the world of our day has little room for idle people, the world of the future will have still less. There are no signs that I can see that society is advancing toward a workless state of existence; when men will be able to live the life of lotus-eaters. In the kind of civilization we have created everybody is needed to put his shoulders to the wheel, and in the higher civilization which is to arise out of this, our posterity shall be more fully employed than we are. The higher our civilization becomes, the more it will demand of us all in the way of vigour, industry, vigilance, skill, and forethought. The challenge of labour is an increasing challenge; the higher powers are not going to make things easier at that point. They will continue in the future as in the past to give society a task proportioned to its powers. As intelligence increases, as science becomes more efficient, as organization becomes more perfect, as liberty becomes more real, we may look out for a corresponding increase in the demand for industry, for courage, for loyalty. To each man according to his several ability. To each age according to its several ability. I see no prospect of a workless civilization—of a state of things when unemployment will be abolished through the abolition of employment, as a wag recently suggested it might be.

What then is leisure? Well, if you look into it you will find this: that our leisure, especially when we are actively following our impulses, *is the time when we are making the greatest demands on the services of our fellow men.* It has been said, with a great deal of truth, that one man's leisure is another man's labour. Our enjoyments, even our refined enjoyments, are possible only because a host of silent workers are providing us with the means for enjoying ourselves. Behind your leisure and mine lies the toil of the silent multitudes. We do well to remember it.

In Mr. Bertrand Russell's book to which I referred in my last lecture, he draws a distinction between labour and leisure of the type I am now criticizing. He treats them as opposites of one another. Labour stands for that part of our life where we are the servants of society, acting under orders. Leisure is that other and better part where we are free men and doing what we please. The object at which we should aim, thinks Mr. Russell, is to reduce the labour, or servant part, to the minimum, and to increase the leisure, or free part, to a maximum. Mr. Russell's view of labour strikes me as somewhat aristocratic, though the book itself, like all his books, is very far from being written in the aristocratic interest. He looks upon labour, on the hammering, and ploughing, and machine-minding, as a necessary nuisance, as so much boredom—he uses that word several times—which nevertheless has to be put up with in order that society may be provided with the necessaries of life. The very opposite, you will observe, to the view taken by Carlyle, who defined labour as the honour and glory of man and the passport to everything that makes life worth living. Mr. Russell thinks further that if science, our great ally, were properly applied to the industrial process, the amount of this drudgery or boredom might be reduced to four hours a day for every man, all the rest becoming leisure in which the worker would be under no man's orders and free to enjoy himself according to his tastes.

Among the leisure occupations which Mr. Russell thinks will become possible when work has been reduced to four hours a day, I note the following,—art, science, thought, contemplation of the universe, enjoyment of the beauties of nature, friendship, and love. Let us look at a few of these leisure occupations and see what they involve.

Art, science, and thought are the most strenuous occupations of man. If you would make good in any of these you must scorn delights and live laborious days! To produce a masterpiece in art, you must go lean for many days and the passers-by will say of you as they said of Dante, "this man surely has been in hell." In the sweat of thy brow, in the sweat of thy brain shalt thou *think*, shalt thou achieve the great discoveries of science, the great creations of art!

Then as to the enjoyment of natural beauty. Would you enjoy a mountain? You must climb it. Would you enjoy the loveliness of the dawn? You must be wide awake and stirring betimes. Would you watch the wild animals at play in the jungle? You must run the risk of being eaten by a lion. Would you behold the majesty of darkness—those mighty apparitions that march across the heavens with the star-diadems on their brows? Then you must watch far into the night, with all your faculties at the stretch, till the glowworm pales his ineffectual fire. There is no laziness in leisure of this kind.

And what shall we say of love, as an occupation for our leisure time? Well! Is not the abode of the beloved mostly guarded by a dragon? Your sword must be sharp, your hand steady, and your heart valiant. Is Hero keeping her lonely vigil on the further shore? You must swim the Hellespont to get there. Is Beatrice waiting your arrival in the earthly Paradise? You must go through hell, and there is no other way. If you are out for the leisure which consists in following your impulses you had better keep clear of all that. "The end of man is an action." Here also the antithesis between labour and leisure completely breaks down.

It comes to this, then. The principle that man's end is an action meets us on every level of life. Met on one level we find that man's life is labour, met on another we find that it is art, science, thought, beauty, human fellowship, and love—the occupations of his so-called leisure. All is of one piece. Leisure is not inaction, but a higher kind of activity. And the problem of our civilization, as I conceive it, is not to reduce labour in favour of leisure—Mr. Russell's method—but to raise labour to those levels of excellence which make it worthy of a man. The transfiguration of labour—the transfiguration of it from a burden that crushes him into a culture that ennobles him; to start labour from the beginning toward those higher activities in which it should end, so that art, science, love, and religion instead of standing aloof from it and apart from it, may come down into it and make it their own. A tremendous problem—a task for giants! But that fine creature whose measure was taken by Aristotle can tackle it—a being not made for the paltry business of hunting after happiness and whining because he cannot find it, but for undertaking distant enterprises, and bearing heavy strains, and embarking on operations of great scope and majesty.

In the next lecture I shall ask how are we to make a beginning. My subject will be Education.

EDUCATION

THE value of rights, in a free democracy, is, we saw, strictly contingent on their subsequent development into duties. Unless this development takes place the rights which the citizen has won are a social danger, for they are apt to become a means in his hand for exercising over others the tyranny from which he has escaped himself. It is only as rights and duties are viewed in relation to one another that either have their full significance. Duties, we may say, are developed rights; rights are the growing points of duties.

This holds, in the first place, of individual citizens, or classes of citizens, within the nation. But it holds equally of the nation as a whole. A nation, for example, which has won the right of self-determination will not reap the fruit of it until that great acquisition expands into a corresponding duty to all the nations by which it is surrounded. A group of free nations, each standing firm on its own right to self-determination, but without expanding these rights into a system of international duty, would be in perpetual danger of war. This is the meaning of that profound saying of Mr. Wilson—that America, just because she is so

great, powerful, and free, is called, not to dominate, but to serve mankind. It was the vision of a
right expanded into a duty.

When, within the nation, some class or classes
of citizens have won their rights, their attention
naturally turns in the first instance to "the down-
trodden multitudes" around them whose lot is less
fortunate than their own. It follows that the first
expansion of right into duty, among the emanci-
pated classes generally, takes the form of fighting
for the rights of their unemancipated fellow countrymen. This expansion is proceeding with great
vigour in all industrial societies at the present
moment, more perhaps on the economic than on
the political field.

Let us assume it completed. Let us throw ourselves forward in imagination to the point when
the rights of all, both economic and political, are
fully secured. What next? Are the rights in question, now become universal, to remain arrested
at that stage? If so, the conditions are barren. As
before the value of the rights strictly depends on
their subsequent expansion into duties. What
form, then, will this expansion take, when reform
has achieved its object of conferring upon every
member of the community his full rights, economic as well as political, as a free man in a free
society?

The ultimate and summary right of every individual is unquestionably the right to self-development. Whatever emancipations we may desire for him, whatever opportunities we may confer upon him, have meaning and value just in so far as they put him in a position to develop himself. This position, which is his right, we now assume that he has already won. We see him, and the whole community to which he belongs, at the critical point when this fundamental right, now completely his, must either expand into a corresponding duty or become a worthless, perhaps a pernicious, possession.

There need be no hesitation in taking the next step. Unless the right to self-development immediately expands into the duty of promoting the self-development of others, the man (or the community) which possesses that right is worse off with it that he would be without it. The ultimate objective of all societies that are advancing on the path of freedom is reciprocal education. Education, interpreted in the widest sense as a social process, national in its first integration, international in its final integration, becomes the summary duty of a civilized world, in which all rights find their issue, and short of which they lose their value. The final form of human society, so far as our minds are able to conceive it, is a world-wide coöperation for the development of man. Only so far as our civilization is leading on to this are we entitled to think of it as a station on the road to something better. If it is not leading on to this, but only to the conferring of rights on men and nations unable to translate them into the corresponding duty, we must conclude that our civilization is a station on the road to something worse.

To the student of social phenomena no more interesting line of inquiry now lies open than that which concerns the relation of the idea of *education* to the idea of *government*. At the moment these two ideas stand in the field as rival claimants for the place of first principle in determining the fortunes of civilization.

That good government is the first need of mankind has long been the accepted faith of political philosophy. But of late a voice has been heard that interprets the primary need in terms of education. "Create good government," say the advocates of the first position, "and education will naturally become a department of its activities." "Educate mankind," say the advocates of the second, "and the need for government will shrink to the minimum and settle itself." At the moment the antagonism of the two claims is only beginning to be felt. But if the demand for education increases, as there is every promise that it will do, the

Dean Inge has remarked that in spite of all the experiments that have been made since civilization began the problem of government has never been solved. We have indeed devised systems and institutions which, when set out on paper, look as though they would work to perfection. What can be simpler that the system which promises self-government by the easy device of choosing *representatives* to do our bidding. But every man is a unique creation, and to suppose that another man can "represent" him is to ignore a fundamental truth of human nature. A host of delusions and fallacies has gathered at this point, too intricate to be investigated here, but well worth investigation. Suffice it to say that they furnish the astute politician with a wardrobe of useful disguises under which, arrayed as a "representative of the people," he can devote himself to the furtherance of sectional interests or even achieve his own fortunes. So far we have found no means of guarding democratic institutions from that kind of misuse. Our systems, even when theoretically perfect, have a way of falling into the hands of imperfect men who often use them for purposes very different from those they were intended to serve. At that point the problem of government remains unsolved, and so will remain, until our politicians, along with the rest of us, have learned to translate their rights into duties. To effect that translation —to complete the rights, both of those who "represent" and those who are "represented," by developing them into duties—is the social function which education, interpreted in the widened sense, has to fulfil. Unsupported by a system of education which has *that* for its ultimate objective, democracy is likely to prove, of all forms of government, the most disastrous.

This consideration alone is enough to indicate the need of a synthesis in which government and education become parts of a unitary operation. Our next step will bring them yet closer together.

The responsibilities of the citizen in a free democracy take two forms, easily distinguished in thought but inseparable in practice. The first is the responsibility for the conscientious employment of the political powers entrusted to him— or in plainer speech, the right use of his vote. A most important affair. But behind that lies a responsibility of far greater importance, one, I am afraid, which our modern democracies have not yet bound up their loins to fulfil. I mean the responsibility, the duty, of *creating values that are worth voting for,* the building up of interests which will give to every citizen who votes a feeling of the worth-whileness of what he is about. The worth-whileness of the thing voted for—

what is the significance of voting apart from that? What does democracy amount to if the things voted for are only the minor interests of the community while the major interests are left to take care of themselves? Teach men the right use of their votes by all means; but, in heaven's name, give them something worth voting for. Picture a community where the vote had been given to everybody who could rightfully claim it, and every voter had been educated to this point of political responsibility, but where the elections all turned on relatively insignificant questions. That would be somewhat of a farce.

I am far from saying that the questions we are asked to vote on are worth nothing. They are generally worth something. But one cannot help wishing they were worth more. We have recently had an election in England. We were all ready and eager to vote on the questions that matter most, on things that are supremely and ultimately worth while—the reconciliation of a distracted world, the promotion of a higher culture, the building up of a firmer friendship between Great Britain and the United States, which many of us regard as supremely and ultimately worth while —but instead of that we were asked to vote on a fiscal problem, important enough if viewed in detachment but insignificant in comparison with problems of greater scope that are clamouring for decision. On the whole, there can be little doubt that the growth of value, of worth-whileness, in the things voted for by democracies has not kept pace with the extension of the voting power. Somehow these voting operations of ours, salutary as they are within their own limits, leave us with a disappointing sense that the things that matter most are precisely those for which, amid the turmoil of secondary interests, we seldom get a chance of voting.

Behind the responsibility we all have for the right use of our votes I suggest, therefore, the existence of a greater responsibilty, that of defining the values that are worth voting for, and bringing them into the foreground of public life. It would be a terrible tragedy if, along with this vast accession of voting power, there should be a decline in the worth-whileness of the things voted on. There are certain laws in this matter which there is no evading. One is that with every decline in the worth-whileness of election programmes you get a parallel decline in democratic leadership—second-rate men for second-rate programmes. Another is that the lower the values for which democracy is working, the more quarrelsome will be the spirit in which they are worked for. The pursuit of wealth and power, for example, is an inherently quarrelsome occupation. Between men and nations with no values in view beyond the right to pursue these things amicable relations cannot exist—no matter what social systems you set up nor what compact or league you enter into. When picking pockets is the business in hand three men will be more peaceable under three umbrellas than under one.

The conclusions to which these considerations lead us may be summarized as follows: the value of government in a free democracy is strictly conditioned by the value of the objects for which the citizens are asked to record their votes. Whether these objects are high or low depends in turn on the degree and kind of education under which the citizens are trained. Under these circumstances good government without good education is impossible.

A second step has now been accomplished in the approach of our two conceptions, government and education. The third brings them into yet more intimate relations.

Allusion has been made above to 'self-government' as the reconciling term which combines the political and the educational activities of a free people.

In most discussions of this hyphenated noun that I am acquainted with, little attention has been paid to the profound change of meaning effected in the idea of government by the addition to it of that modest prefix 'self.' The assumption commonly is that the only difference between self-government and government by not-self—*i.e.*, by external authority, by the imposed will of another —is a transference in the seat of authority. Under self-government a man is his own master, a nation is its own master; the mastership is within, and not, as under a tyranny, without. Under either system the range of duty is the same; the difference being that in the former case our duties are self-imposed, in the latter, imposed by another. Such is the common assumption.

The truth is that under self-government the range of duty becomes enormously expanded, and the character of duty so changed, or transfigured, that it becomes a question whether the word 'government' is any longer applicable to the process we have in mind.

A man who undertakes to govern himself must not only think of himself as *exercising* the government, but must also think of himself—of his total self—as the *object on which* the government has to be exercised. He is object as well as subject. To be self-governing, he must have his total self under control. To call a man self-governed because he was his own master in the use of his vote, or in any other selected activity, while the rest of his powers and faculties, his private habits and his human relationships in general, were subject to no law but that of caprice, would be the greatest of absurdities. Apart from this double meaning the word has no meaning at all. Our self-governed man is master of himself not only in the sense that his total self conducts the government but in the deeper sense that his total self submits to the government so exercised. This deeper meaning of the term is commonly overlooked.

As with self-governing individuals, so with self-governing nations. A nation has not achieved self-government until it has the whole range of its interests—its total self—completely in hand. It is not enough that it should be able to claim that what laws it has are self-imposed. It must be able to claim further that all the essential currents of its life are law-abiding. Kings and tyrants may confine themselves to protecting the lives and property of their subjects. But a *self*-governing nation must be master of its own soul. That the citizens make their own laws for the protection of life and property may be the necessary first step. But it is no more than that. If the arts and sciences are left to take their chance, if the growth of knowledge and the formation of character are uncontrolled to any purpose or by any ideal—to predi-

cate self-government of a nation in that condition
would be an absurdity no less flagrant than in the
parallel case of the individual just considered.
Whether it knows this or not the nation which
adopts self-government embarks on a vast educational enterprise which will not be complete, or on
the way to completion, until self-government has
been transfigured into self-development.

Such is the immense expansion of scope which
the duties of the citizen undergo when the idea of
self-government is made the basis of the political
creed. There is no stopping short of the stage
when education will become the chief business
of the state. At this point the fusion of the idea
of government with the idea of education, a point
far in the future, no doubt, but inevitable, becomes complete. The right of self-determination,
possessed by each, has expanded into the duty of
reciprocal culture, in which all participate.

The objection will be rightly made that the
vision which these considerations bring before the
mind is too distant to be of any value as a working theory under present conditions. Our thought
needs to be grounded on a nearer vision of what
education is, or ought to be, under the actual conditions of industrial civilization. To this matter

I now address myself. What is "education"? Or (if the term be preferred) what is "culture"?

The question was answered in terms that have now become classical by Matthew Arnold. Culture, as he defined it, is "the study of perfection," or "getting to know . . . the best which has been thought and said."

In common with Carlyle, Matthew Arnold believed that industrial civilization was drifting toward "anarchy," and the fifty-odd years that have elapsed since *Culture and Anarchy* was written, with the Great War and its terrible sequel at the end of them, have certainly brought no mitigation of the dangers against which these two prophets lifted up their warning voices. It was in "culture" as defined above that Arnold found the only defence of our civilization against the "anarchy" to which it would otherwise drift. To the various programmes of "the political operators" he attached little importance, regarding them for the most part as deceitful "claptrap," which served no purpose save the malign one of diverting the attention of the public from the real sources of human well-being. To get rid of this "claptrap"—Carlyle called it "cant"—to free ourselves from the fatal "stock notions" that are obsessing us, to understand the realities of the world—we must have "culture," we must "study perfection," we must "get to know the best which has been thought and said."

Arnold's defence of culture—of education—as the sole means possessed by modern society for averting the anarchy which threatens it, which earned him the title of "the elegant Jeremiah," stands in principle, as sound today as when it was first uttered. But his definition of "culture" is inadequate and calls for amendment.

Accepting the word "industrial" as correctly describing the essential character of our civilization, it follows, obviously and immediately, that the education appropriate to these conditions will turn on the *industry* by which that civilization lives, and in which it has its being. An education which teaches mankind all else it may be desirable to know but leaves it untaught in respect to the industry which is the breath of its nostrils, is clearly inappropriate to industrial civilization. If such a civilization is to be educated at all it must be educated in and through its industry—taking this term as including the whole sum of functions involved in carrying on the work of civilization from day to day—an inclusion, it may be remarked, which covers the fine arts as well as the lowest form of unskilled labour. To see the inadequacy of Arnold's definition we have only to contemplate a community whose members are engaged occasionally and for short periods in "getting to know the best which has been thought and said" and continuously and for long periods in doing monotonous work which exhausts the body without interesting the mind. Under these circumstances, culture would be no more than a "beneficent extra." Education would be pulling in one direction with a feeble force and industry would be pulling in the opposite direction with a mighty force.

These considerations lead us at once to the definition of education we are in search of. *Education is the process of training the industry of man, in its manifold varieties, and in its organized totality, to the highest pitch of excellence it is capable of attaining*. The only type of education appropriate to an industrial civilization must be conceived in these terms. It will have its roots in the actual labour of mankind and will return into that labour to endow it with higher qualities and more valuable aims. As the guiding principle of the educator, in these times, as the ultimate objective of his endeavours, nothing short of this can be offered.

Two objections will immediately occur.

1. In the first place it will be said that the true aim of education is not the excellence of the work done but the excellence of the man who does it.

something else. In others it depends on economic considerations—whether you have this system or that. With others again it is all a question of propaganda, what the churches are saying, what the brilliant writers are saying, what the speech-makers are saying. These are secondary causes, important enough in their proper place, but not the root of the matter. The root of the matter lies not in what the people are *saying,* but in what they are *doing,* and in how they are doing it, "in the quality of our striving," as Goethe said. It lies in the value of the service which each one of us is contributing through his vocation, through his daily work, to the general task of carrying society on from day to day. So long as the majority of mankind are engaged in work that is not worthy of them, or so long as they are doing worthy work in an unworthy manner, education will be defeated, and the excellence of man will not appear.

2. "But what," it will be asked, "is to become of learning and scholarship; of morality and religion; of literature, poetry, and all the arts which give dignity and beauty to life? These are the ultimate values, and nothing can be worthy the name of education, of culture, which fails to concentrate its efforts on promoting them. But if culture, as you are now suggesting, becomes yoked to industry, if education is to be "married to

has drifted aside into the position of a "beneficent extra," out of relation to the main interests of human life, and impotent to affect the main currents of civilization, which, meanwhile, are slowly gliding on their way, if the wisest of modern prophets may be trusted, to anarchy and the bottomless pit. What is here suggested is in fact nothing less than this: that industrial civilization must either find a means of ending the divorce between its industry and its "culture" or perish in the alternative. No doubt it is a task for giants. But the race of giants, even in this dwarfish age, is not entirely extinct.

Nor is any contempt here involved toward the "best which has been thought and said"—the great literature, the great art, of the past. But we are profoundly concerned that the present generation, and still more the next, should find in their age, as our fathers and forerunners found in theirs, the subject matter for noble thinking and for noble speech. We dread the coming of a time when the labour of man will have sunk to a condition of mechanical monotony, when nothing noble remains either to think or say about it, and when the only achievements worthy of great thought and great speech will be the achievements of long-buried generations. To know the best which *has been* thought and said is certainly good; but to be engaged in actions and achievements which

prompt those who behold them to a profounder
thinking and a more beautiful utterance, is certainly far better. We must not forget that behind
all the great literature and great art of the past,
there lay a background of great *work* achieved
by the nation or race amid which the poets and
the artists were born. A civilization whose culture
is confined to "knowing" what these artists and
poets have done, but which takes no pains to furnish its own artists and poets with equally significant themes, is like a husbandman who consumes
a harvest that has been reaped but sows nothing
for next year's crop. It is living on its capital.

"I call, therefore, a complete and generous education," says Milton, "that which fits a man to
perform justly, skilfully and magnanimously all
the offices, both private and public, of peace and
war."

"The offices, both public and private of peace
and war," have assumed in these days a character very different from that of the time when those
words were written. But the essential truth of
them stands unchanged. If it can be recovered—
and many minds are now busy in recovering it—
the prospects of industrial civilization, now so
gloomy, will glow with a new light of hope. Short
of this recovered ideal, short of the marriage of

labour and education which it foreshadows, I
know of nothing which can justify the belief that
industrial civilization is 'a station on the road to
something better.' No danger is involved that men
will forget the "best which has been thought and
said." Under the conditions we are imagining "the
study of perfection" will lead to the practice of
it, in a continual effort to lift the labour of mankind to the highest level of excellence it is capable of reaching. The ethics of workmanship, long
despised and neglected, will be restored to its
place, and the "well doing of everything that
needs to be done" will become the policy of states
and the supreme responsibility of the citizen. As
the quality of work rises to higher levels the mind
will discover new themes for thought, the tongue
and the pen new themes for utterance; and in the
thoughts thus arising, and in the speech that follows them, "the best which has been thought and
said" will be bettered. The arts and the moralities
will revive. Religion also. Through the pursuit of
excellence our civilization will find the way, which
it has now lost, to the Supreme Excellence, whom
we call God. There is no other way.

INTERNATIONAL TRUSTEESHIP

AMONG thoughtful men whom I have had the good fortune to meet in this country, and I have met not a few since I came over, I observe there is grave concern as to the fate in store for western civilization. The same concern is felt in my own country. The pace of civilization is growing faster and faster, the mass-momentum is increasing, but nobody seems to know where we are going. Wise men are growing anxious. We are in the rapids.

Is western civilization—industrial civilization as it has now become—on the right road, or on the wrong? Is it a station on the way to something better or a station on the way to something worse?

I find opinion sharply divided, even among the most careful observers of both countries. Some of them are profoundly pessimistic. Others are equally optimistic. Others again oscillate between the two extremes—hopeful today and despondent tomorrow. My own mind oscillates in this manner, and never more so than when I am in America. There are some features in the life I observe here that fill one with hope for the future. Your idealism is unbounded and your idealists mean busi-

ness. Other features cause the gravest alarm. You
are growing dangerously rich. To decide whether
western civilization is on the right road or the
wrong is not easy.

There are, however, a few points on which one
may feel reasonably confident.

Whether we are on the right road or the wrong
depends on ourselves. Given a united will to do it,
I believe we can make a human success of industrial civilization. But if things are allowed to drift
and take their own course, the love of pleasure
and of money as a means to pleasure will undo
us and we will come to no good end.

Again, there are only two alternatives, so far as
I can see, before us. Our civilization will end
either in the greatest triumph or in the greatest
disaster the world has ever seen. Either we are on
the road to some far-off divine event; or we are
on the road to catastrophe. This last was the
opinion of Carlyle. Sixty years ago he prophe-
sied that our civilization would end in ruin—or,
as he called it, "the bottomless pit." He thought
it would take about three generations to bring us
there; and that time has nearly elapsed. His essay
on "Shooting Niagara" is well worth reading at
the present time. It contains some prophecies
which have already come true in the Great War
and in its consequences. It contains other prophe-

cies which have not come true, and let us hope never will. But his warnings are not to be lightly disregarded.

The third point on which I feel pretty certain is this. Whatever destination industrial society is moving toward, whether a good one or a bad one, America will get there first. You are making the pace for the whole world. In America things are moving to their issues faster than they are anywhere else. The drag of old traditions, which slackens the pace in Europe, affects you little in this country.

The fourth bears directly on my general subject. Western civilization is a unitary thing which stands or falls together. The fate of the whole will be the fate of the parts. There is not one fate in store for America and another for Europe. Whatever happens to the one will happen sooner or later to the other.

That leads me to the strongest argument that I know of for a League of Nations. It is the unity of western civilization. As nations we are separated from one another, but in our civilization we are all one. We are one in our culture and our ethical standards, and these are the things that make civilization worth preserving and life worth living for all of us.

I said a moment ago that whether we come to a

good end or a bad one depends on ourselves. If western civilization is to be saved from the terrible disasters that threaten it, all nations must coöperate to save it. If it is to be victorious, as I believe it will be, all nations must coöperate to make it so. They must pool their resources, especially their resources of good-will, of intellect, and of education. They must find a ground of union somewhere and somehow, where the best qualities of all nations, the best men of all nations, can act together for the common good. Whether that ground of union exists in the League of Nations as at present constituted may be a question. But if it doesn't exist there, we must find another, and a better, means of acting together. Either that will be done, or the terrible prophecies of Carlyle and of others will come true. There will be a disaster for all of us.

I regard the League of Nations as the most difficult enterprise on which the good-will of the Christian nations has ever embarked. The most difficult, but the most promising, the most fruitful, the most splendid, the most worth while. If freedom consists in willing subjection to an end that is worth while, here surely is an end to which the free man may consecrate his life. But let him be under no illusion as to the difficulties before him. The League of Nations cannot be talked into existence. It cannot be created by writing books on it, or by giving lectures on it, as I am doing now. There is hard work ahead for any man who takes up that enterprise, and hard fighting, too, not of course with carnal weapons, but with spiritual weapons, with the sword of the spirit. We need courage like that of Sir Galahad when he set out to find the Holy Grail.

The difficulties of the enterprise, far from being a reason for giving it up in despair, are, to my mind, a reason for accepting it as the challenge of Christianity to our day and generation. Christianity is always a challenge—a challenge to take up a cross and follow the Master along difficult roads. Christianity flings at our feet tasks that are seemingly impossible, tasks that look fantastic to the natural man, and says to us "do that!" The natural man runs away from these difficult things. The spiritual man takes them up and wins the victory that overcomes the world. It is the spiritual man that Christianity addresses when it calls us to create a fraternity of nations.

The League of Nations is an enterprise which calls for long-sustained and heroic endeavours, for constant forbearance in our attitude to other nations and for a great power of facing reverses

before the end is reached. Most of the disappoint-
ments which its advocates have endured up to
date are due to an underestimate of the difficulties, to the attempt to reach by the short-cut of a
political covenant ends which can only be reached
by long and arduous journeys toward other points
of the compass.

A long road has to be travelled before the great
aristocratic nations can be induced to submit their
national power and pride of place to any kind of
international discipline. All nations are aristocratic on the field of foreign politics, however
democratic they may be in their inner constitu-
tion. When the phrase about 'making the world
safe for democracy' was invented it was not sufficiently realized that every great nation, in its
national self-consciousness and in its attitude to
other nations, is as proud as Lucifer. The spirit of
democracy has done its work on the internal
structures of the democratic nations. It has
hardly affected their external relationships to one
another. These remain on an aristocratic basis.
Foreign policy is always an affair between aris-
tocrats. When two democratic nations, say England and France, negotiate with one another on a
question of foreign policy, the negotiators are two
proud aristocracies, abnormally sensitive on the
point of national honour, and unwilling to yield

on any point which touches that. To suppose that these mighty powers, these *grands seigneurs* of the international world, will consent at a bound to submit to the discipline of majority voting, in which small or undeveloped nations have equal voting rights with themselves, is to ignore the whole psychology of nationalism. Yet that is what making the world safe for democracy implies. It means not merely securing to each nation the right to be as democratic as it pleases within its own borders, but something far more difficult— the introduction of the democratic principle into the relation of states and empires on the field of foreign policy.

If the work of the League of Nations up to date be examined it will be found that progress stops at the point when the aristocratic instincts of nationalism stand affected. Yet these are the very points where the dangers arise that threaten the peace of the world. The aristocratic instincts of nationalism are at this moment the chief obstacles which bar the way of those who would make the world safe for democracy. They are as strong in your country as they are in my own. There is no prouder nation on earth than the American, and I doubt if you would have it otherwise. You have something to be proud of. I cannot conceive this great nation submitting, any more than I can con-

ceive my own submitting, to have its international
behaviour regulated and disciplined by a system
of majority voting, in which small, immature, and
inexperienced nations would have equal voting
rights with itself.

In the democratic system as we have adopted
it in Britain my scullery maid and I have equal
voting rights; and though the arrangement is
somewhat offensive to my sense of my own importance I consider it good for the scullery maid
and submit to it accordingly. If it results, as Dean
Inge thinks it will, in the class to which I belong
being ultimately voted out of existence, I should
not regard that as a fatal objection to it, since I
do not think that I and the likes of me are indispensable to the maintenance of human society.
But a long road has to be travelled before you can
persuade the United States or the British Empire
to adopt the attitude in this matter to Honduras,
or Hayti, or Paraguay, that I have learnt to adopt
toward my scullery maid. That is one sample of
the difficulties that confront us, an indication of
the long road to be travelled, before we can estab-
lish a League of Nations on a democratic basis,
and so make the world safe for democracy in that
large international sense.

Another difficulty arises from the constant
changes of *personnel* that takes place in demo-

cratic governments, from the breaks and interruptions to which they are exposed through the rise and fall of parties, through the ups and downs of electioneering conditions. To solve the problem of international good-will you need a long period of continuous endeavour carried on as far as possible by the same individuals, undisturbed by the vicissitudes of elections, and able to give an undivided attention to the great task before them. But if the business has to be carried on today by men with one set of principles, and tomorrow by men with another set, all continuity of action will be lost. The distant object at which you are aiming will be sacrificed for something more showy, which satisfies the electors and strengthens the position of the party in power for the time being. This has happened already. It happened, for example, when Signor Mussolini, whom a sudden change of feeling had brought into power, refused to submit the Italian quarrel with Greece to the terms of the covenant which his predecessor, Signor Nitti, had signed.

The first step to the accomplishment of the end we desire is *the creation of an international public opinion,* and of proper organs for expressing it, of sufficient weight and authority to act as a guide in common action and as a restraining force at dangerous conjunctures. At the present moment no such thing exists, there is no international public opinion, and for want of that, the decisions of the League of Nations, whenever they touch the major problems I have just been speaking of, lack the driving power which would make them effective. In the nations taken one by one public opinion on foreign affairs may assume a fairly consistent form, but the public opinion of one nation is unrelated to that of others, so that the totality forms a chaos, in which a sound opinion in one state is cancelled by the unsound opinion in another, and nothing decisive can be done.

In addition to which we have to reckon with the fact—the sinister fact—that even such public opinion as exists in foreign policy is very largely at the mercy of an irresponsible newspaper press, a power of the first magnitude, which no democracy has yet learnt to control. As things now are, it is impossible for any responsible statesman to advance a proposal for a better understanding between nations without encountering from the newspaper press a hostile interpretation of his proposal, which represents it as a subtle move in the game of national self-interest. In this way a spirit of mistrust is introduced which poisons international relationships, and breeds suspicion at the very points where mutual confidence between the parties is essential. Mr. Lloyd George, returning from the Conference of Genoa, declared that in the atmosphere of mutual mistrust which he had found prevailing there, largely the work of the newspaper press, effective action was barred from the outset. To make head against this deplorable state of things, the first step must obviously be the creation of an international public opinion which can speak with an authority greater than that of any single nation and of the newspapers which represent or misrepresent it. Can this be done?

It could be done if one half the attention and thought were devoted to the matter which were given to devising the political machinery embodied in the covenant of the League of Nations. I am not going to criticize that machinery, on which perhaps you have heard more than enough, except on the general ground that in these days we attach too much importance to the machine and too little to the moral forces that are needed to work it. We are making that mistake all along the line, and we reap the consequences of it when we see our democratic machinery captured by sinister interests which use the machine for purposes clean opposite to those for which it was intended. In the covenant of the League of Nations you have a highly complicated piece of machinery, faulty at points no doubt, but bearing witness on the whole to the immense skill of those who created it. But the moral forces that could set it working, the international public opinion which could make it effective at the critical points, is unorganized and virtually non-existent. There is a lion in the path at this point, and he must be got rid of before we can advance.

In describing what I have in mind I ask you to attach no importance to names that I use, which are merely provisional and perhaps not the best that could be chosen. I shall probably find better ones as I get more light on the subject from the criticism of those who are in sympathy with the main idea. What I care for is the idea; the names are nothing.

Briefly, then. I am looking forward to the creation of an International Court of Appeal, or, as I prefer to call it an International Court of Honour, the members of which shall be International Trustees, chosen for life from the wisest and best of all nations.

I will speak first of the International Trustees, for the significance of what I am about to urge hinges primarily on the character of the persons who would be the responsible agents in carrying it on. Their character is summed up in the word 'trusteeship.' Trusteeship rather than diplomacy. It is a distant object we are aiming at, and the first step toward its attainment is to avoid the politician, with his short and precarious tenure of power, his electioneering entanglements, his arts and his manœuvres, and to fill his place by the life-Trustee, a type of person with far higher qualifications for the work in hand.

In all the civilized nations of today men are to be found who have the broad interests of humanity at heart. Without sacrifice of their national characteristics they are yet possessed of the international mind; men whose *bona fides* is above suspicion, holding an established position not only in the esteem of their fellow countrymen but in the esteem of foreigners as well. Such men could be found at no great distance from the spot where I am now standing; and if here, then elsewhere also. Very few of these are in politics; but their influence outside of politics is immense, and not confined to their own countries; men who understand the world in which we are living, wise, great-hearted and magnanimous. Names are floating through my mind as I speak, and perhaps through yours also. They are the names of men whose fortunes are not at the mercy of the newspaper press; men whose minds have not been diverted from the paths of justice and humanity

by electioneering compromise. These are the men
we need to dissipate the malign atmosphere of
mistrust which poisons foreign policy, to lay the
foundations of an international ethic, which at
present does not exist, and to create an international public opinion. Difficulties as to the method
of choosing them would no doubt arise; but they
are not insuperable; and I cannot but believe that
these difficulties would be overcome when once
the nations were awake to the necessity of choosing their wisest and best as Trustees for international work. They should be chosen for life, or
for the effective part of life, and their appoint-
ment should be one of the highest honours which
the state confers upon its citizens. Their office
would be that of International Trustees.

In their totality these Trustees would constitute
an International Court of Honour. No physical
forces would be at their disposal, to threaten the
sovereign rights of nations, and so provoke the
very kind of quarrel it was intended to suppress.
They would deliberate continuously; they would
issue reports at regular intervals; they would
have their own means of publicity; and at dangerous moments they would declare their findings
on the rights and wrongs of the case. In course of
time these findings would acquire authority; and
a point would be reached when any nation which

League of Nations as now constituted. That may
or may not be a good thing for you to do. But the
decision must come from your own initiative and
not from the pleadings of others. I am concerned
with something different. I am pleading for another line of action which leaves the present
League of Nations unaffected and free to grow
to whatever issues may be awaiting it—action on
a higher level, where, if I rightly understand what
I am talking about, the American genius is pecu-
liarly fitted to play a leading part. There is in
this country a fund of human kindness, a fund
of humanitarianism, such as few nations have possessed. I reckon it among the greatest of your
natural assets and I think that a day will come
when this humanitarianism of yours will mobilize
itself into a motive force for promoting the friendship of all nations. Someone has said—I think
it was George Santayana—that whenever he met
a man who had no kindness of heart, he knew
that man was not an American. It is a fact of
immense international significance, and it is in
that connection that I speak of it now. It means
that when the question arises of taking international action on humanistic lines, and that in my
opinion is the most hopeful line on which it can
be taken, it is natural to look to you to take a

lead. That is the reason for the confidence I feel in bringing these matters before you today.

It is the misfortune of all nations, that their best qualities are apt to become sterilized by passing through the official medium of their foreign offices. The nations need a meeting ground where they can hold intercourse in their true character, and not as the mere abstractions, or as the monsters and bogeys which they become to one another under the distortions and manœuvrings of foreign policy. Were such a meeting point to be created the fund of kindness in the American character would begin to assert itself as a world force of incalculable value. There are qualities in other nations, too, to which it would not appeal in vain. Most men are better than their principles. Most nations are better than their foreign policies.

Fantastic as this proposal may appear there are times when I am tempted to think that it has already begun to realize itself—not under the names I have used, nor directly, but by indirection. I attach especial importance to the movement already begun, which is drawing the great educational centers of the world, the universities, a little nearer together. From the drawing together of the universities I look for the breaking out of a great light on the international problem, a light which shall also be an actuating power. The universities are growing points for the solidarity of mankind. In them will be bred the International Trustees of the future, the men who understand the human values for which international trustee-ship is necessary. I do not hesitate to say that the greatest men now living are educators. An insight has come to many of them that the ultimate aims of education, which are as wide as humanity, can only be pursued through international coöpera-tion. Among the leading educators of the nations men might be found at once fully qualified for the part of International Trustees. Others would come from the judicial bench. Others would be men who had already proved themselves in fiduci-ary positions in the business and financial world. Others would be labour men.

The creation of an international ethic is not to be brought about by fitful outbursts of propa-ganda, by a treatise on the subject written here or there, by isolated efforts in theory, no matter how convincingly argued. It can come about only through the actual exercise of the ethical judg-ment of the nations on concrete ethical situations, as they arise one by one. For that purpose an ap-propriate organ is needed. I have called it an International Court of Honour. But I imagine that such a Court would soon find that questions of honour could not be decided without a general reference to the wider interests of mankind. The decisions of any point in international ethics would carry with it far-reaching implications, which would affect all ethics whatsoever, not excepting those by which we regulate the conduct of our private lives. An educational enterprise, beneficently affecting all nations would be set on foot, the end of which no man could forsee.

I will now sum up the main points on which, as it seems to me, attention needs to be focussed.

1. The forces to which we must look to create a League of Nations are ethical, judicial, educational, fiduciary, and religious. These are the forces we should seek to combine in order to secure the coöperative action of well-disposed nations for the common good of mankind.

2. The League established by the covenant of 1919, which the United States has not joined, is a League of *Governments* rather than a League of *Nations*. A League of Nations is a much larger enterprise than a League of Governments. To create it we must combine the highest elements in the nations concerned. These highest elements are not always represented by the official governments in power for the time being. But they exist, and men to represent them can be found—our International Trustees.

3. The official governments of the world are all established and carried on in the interests of nationalism, and each of them is bound to consider its sovereign rights as paramount. This makes combined action on international lines extremely difficult, when the acting parties are the governments in question. But combined action of the kind I have been pleading for is not obstructed by this difficulty. There may be weighty reasons, reasons of sovereign rights, why the United States should hold back from joining a League of Governments. But I do not imagine that the American nation would hesitate for a moment to lend its best and wisest men, its highest talent in the judicial, educational, fiduciary, and religious field, for the purpose of creating an international public opinion, in favour of peace, coöperation, and good-will.

4. The first move in this direction might very well originate in the universities, more especially in the universities of your nation and mine, whose relations are already those of mutual good-will and coöperation, and are becoming more intimate through frequent interchange of learning, through the Rhodes Scholarships, and through increased intercommunication in general. The movement would have to extend far beyond the universities

before it could be successful, but a starting point
has to be found somewhere, and this is the most
promising I can think of.

5. In appointing the Trustees to do the work
I have outlined, the action of government would
no doubt have to be invoked. This is not a fatal
difficulty. A government which appoints judges
for life, and appoints them on a non-partisan
basis, is competent to appoint International Trustees in the same manner, provided always that
public opinion is on the watch, as it is in the case
of the judges, to prevent such appointments going
to any but the best men.

With that I leave the matter to your reflection
and your criticism. As I said at the beginning,
western civilization is unquestionably at the cross-
roads. And there are only two of them. One leads
to the victory of mankind; the other leads to
disaster. If we are to gain the victory we must
pool our moral resources. The situation will not
brook indefinite delay. It may get out of hand
and rush to ruin with a speed that nothing can
stop. Some means must be found for bringing the
moral forces together in advance of the catas-
trophes that threaten us.

I think the lead will have to come from your
nation and mine. I know what the difficulties are,

I have not read history quite for nothing. But this I will venture to say. If your nation and mine cannot work together in this matter I do not know what other two nations can.